IT'S AMAZING!
SUPERHEROES

Annabel Savery

W
FRANKLIN WATTS
LONDON • SYDNEY

This edition 2013

First published in 2011 by
Franklin Watts
338 Euston Road
London NW1 3BH

Franklin Watts Australia
Level 17/207 Kent Street
Sydney NSW 2000

© 2011 Franklin Watts

Planning and production by Discovery Books Limited
Managing editor: Laura Durman
Editor: Annabel Savery
Designer: Ian Winton

Picture credits: Alamy: p. 4 (AF Archive), p. 7 bottom (Pictorial Press Ltd), p. 9
(AF Archive), p. 10 (AF Archive), p. 17 (AF Archive), p. 23 (Photos 12), p. 25
(Photos 12), p. 28 (Moviestore Collection Ltd); Getty Images: p. 6; Photoshot:
p. 5 (Starstock), p. 8, p. 11 (Starstock), p. 13, p. 14, p. 16, p. 18 (Starstock), p. 19,
p. 22, p. 24, p. 26, p. 29; Shutterstock Images: p. 7 top (all Carsten Reisinger),
p. 27 top and p. 31 (Faiz Zaki), p. 27 bottom (DDCoral); Cartoon Network: Title,
p. 20 left, p. 20 right, p. 21 (BEN 10 and all related elements are TM and ©
Cartoon Network. All rights reserved.)

Cover: IstockPhoto.com: serow.

Every attempt has been made to clear copyright. Should there be any
inadvertent omission, please apply to the publisher for rectification.

A CIP catalogue record for this book is available from the British Library.

Dewey Decimal Classification Number: 398.2'2

ISBN: 978 1 4451 1743 0

Franklin Watts is a division of Hachette Children's Books,
an Hachette UK company.
www.hachette.co.uk

Printed in China

CONTENTS

4   What are superheroes?

6   The comics

8   Superman

10   Spider-Man

12   Wonder Woman

14   Batman

16   The Hulk

18   Iron Man

20   Ben 10

22   The Fantastic Four

24   The X-Men

26   Transformers

28   Superhero films

30   Glossary and further information

32   Index

All words in **bold** appear in the glossary on page 30.

WHAT ARE THE HEROES?

Superheroes are people from stories who have special powers. Some of these special powers include being able to fly, being incredibly strong, and being able to heal themselves.

Spider-Man

Superheroes use their powers for good. They help to protect people by solving crimes and catching criminals. Superheroes often rescue people, too (left).

Superheroes get their powers in different ways. They might be born with them, or find they have them after an accident. Other superheroes use **gadgets** to protect themselves and help them to win fights.

Secret identities

Most superheroes have secret identities. They hide their faces when they rescue people so that they cannot be recognised. Bruce Wayne (below) wears his batman costume so that people do not know who Batman really is.

THE COMICS

Most superheroes were originally created for comics. There are two main superhero comic book makers. These are DC and Marvel.

DC and Marvel comic books tell all sorts of exciting adventures of different superheroes. They are written like a **storyboard**, so that you can read them like watching a film.

A Marvel comic book

When the superheroes fight evil criminals, the comics use words like KAPOW, WHAMM, and ZAP to represent the sounds.

So many superheroes

DC and Marvel have created hundreds of superheroes. As well as Superman (see pages 8–9) and Spider-Man (see pages 10–11), other great characters include The Flash, Aquaman and Daredevil (left).

SUPERMAN

Superman's human name is Clark Kent. Although he looks human, he is actually an alien from the planet of Krypton. His alien name is Kal-El.

Superman (below) has many superpowers. He is fast, powerful and can fly. He also has super vision which means he can see through things, and see things that are a long way away.

Kryptonite

There is only one thing that can really hurt Superman – kryptonite. This is a **radioactive mineral** that was created when his home planet was destroyed. It takes away Superman's powers and can even kill him.

Kryptonite

Superman's **nemesis** is Lex Luthor (right). He is a rich scientist who has always hated Superman. He even tries to destroy him using kryptonite.

Spider-Man's real identity is Peter Parker. He was an ordinary boy until he was bitten by a radioactive spider. This gave him spider-like powers.

Spider-Man (above) can shoot webs from his wrists. He uses these to swing from tall buildings and to escape from danger. He can also cling to any surface and use his 'spider senses' to react quickly to danger.

Spider-Man has many enemies, but the main one is the Green Goblin. He is very powerful, but is also **insane**. Other enemies are Dr Octopus (above) and Venom.

Famous words

Spider-Man's famous line is 'With great power comes great responsibility'. It appeared in the first Spider-Man comic.

WONDER WOMAN

Wonder Woman is the most famous female superhero. She is Princess of the Amazons and has many superpowers.

Wonder Woman is super-strong and super-fast. She also has special powers, such as being able to talk to animals and even super-quick typing!

Wonder Woman uses special equipment. She wears silver bracelets that **deflect** bullets. She has a tiara that can be thrown at enemies. She also carries a special rope called the 'Lasso of Truth'. Once inside it, a person cannot escape and can only tell the truth.

IT'S AMAZING!

As well as all her other equipment, Wonder Woman also has an invisible aeroplane!

Silver
bracelet

Lasso
of Truth

13

BATMAN

Batman protects the people of Gotham City. His real name is Bruce Wayne. He is also known as 'The Caped Crusader'.

Bruce Wayne is a very rich man. His strength and power come through training rather than **supernatural** abilities.

Batman wears a special suit made of tough material. He speeds around in an **armoured** car called the Batmobile. It has rocket boosters to make a quick getaway!

The bat-light

When Batman is needed, the Gotham City police shine a searchlight with a bat-symbol into the sky for Batman to see.

Batman's main enemy is the Joker. He is very clever and evil. The Joker tries to kill Batman and the people who are close to him. Batman has other enemies that are just as scary, such as Catwoman and The Riddler.

THE HULK

The Hulk was an ordinary scientist called Dr Bruce Banner until he was accidentally hit by the gamma rays from a bomb.

The bomb turned Bruce Banner into a superhero. When Bruce is angry, he changes into the Hulk (below). The Hulk is enormous and incredibly strong. He is also bright green! The Hulk's strength increases with his temper, but even though he gets angry he is still one of the good guys.

The Hulk's strength is not his only power. He can stand temperatures as hot as the Sun and survive in space or underwater without any equipment. His body also heals itself after an injury.

A nearby nemesis

Bruce Banner has a girlfriend called Betty Ross (below left). Unfortunately, her father is General Ross (below right), the Hulk's arch-enemy.

IRON MAN

The man behind the Iron Man suit is Tony Stark. He is a genius and the owner of a company called Stark Enterprises.

Tony Stark was kidnapped by an enemy, and his captors tried to force him to make them a powerful weapon. Instead, he made the Iron Man suit (right) in secret, and used it to escape. Later, he uses the suit to protect the world from powerful criminals.

Heart-stopping!

When he was kidnapped Tony Stark was injured, and he has to wear a chest plate to keep his heart working. The chest plate is also the battery for the suit.

Battery

The Iron Man suit gives Tony Stark all his power. It is made of very tough material to protect his body. The palms of his hands (above) can fire **repulsor rays** at enemies. The suit also has powerful rocket boosters in the feet so that Iron Man can fly!

BEN 10

Ben 10 is a favourite superhero with kids everywhere!

Ben 10 is the superhero name of a boy called Ben Tennyson (below). Ben uses a wristwatch called an Omnitrix to turn himself into different aliens with superpowers.

Omnitrix

Ben is helped by his Grandpa Max and his cousin Gwen. They go on adventures together. He uses his powers to fight criminals. He often gets into mischief on his adventures, too!

Ben 10 was created in 2005 by a group called 'Man of Action'. The character is so popular that there are now Ben 10 cartoons, films and video games.

Powerful aliens

All of Ben's aliens have superpowers. For example, Nanomech (right) can shrink to a tiny size, fly and shoot blasts of energy.

THE FANTASTIC FOUR

The Fantastic Four are a group of superheroes who work together. They have no secret identities, so everybody knows who they are.

Cosmic rays

Originally the Fantastic Four were space shuttle pilots. They were hit by cosmic rays and their superpowers came from this accident.

Reed Richards – 'Mr Fantastic'

Each of the Fantastic Four has a different superpower. Mr Fantastic can bend himself into any shape. His wife, Susan Storm, is the Invisible Woman and her brother, the Human Torch, can burst into flames and fly. Their friend, the Thing, has stone-like flesh which means he is very strong.

**Johnny Storm –
'The Human Torch'**

**Susan Storm –
'The Invisible Woman'**

**Reed Richards –
'Mr Fantastic'**

**Ben Grim –
'The Thing'**

THE X-MEN

The X-Men are another group of superheroes who work together.

The X-Men's powers come from **genetic mutations**. For example, Wolverine (above centre) was born with animal senses, claws that spring out of his hands and the ability to heal from any injury.

One of the X-Men is Storm (below). She can control the weather, and is a brilliant fighter.

Professor Charles Xavier is the leader of the X-Men and the man who brought them together. He created a training centre for them in his mansion so that they could learn to use their powers for good.

IT'S AMAZING!

To start with there were only five X-Men. Now there are nearly 100!

The Transformers are a group of alien robots.

There are good Transformers and bad Transformers. The Autobots are the good robots and the Decepticons are their enemies.

The Autobots come from a planet called Cybertron. They are led by Optimus Prime. His team of Autobots on Earth are Bumblebee, Ratchett, Ironhide and Jazz.

**Autobot
Optimus Prime**

Both the Autobots and the Decepticons are **humanoid** robots. However, they can transform into machines, such as vehicles or aircraft. Bumblebee (left) transforms into a yellow car (below).

Bumblebee

Toy Transformers

Transformers started as a line of toys made by a company called Hasbro. They were so popular that they were made into Marvel Comics series, cartoons, video games and films.

SU----H-R-- -FILM

Many films have been made about superheroes. Here are some facts about them that you might not know.

The first big superhero film was about Superman (above). It was made in 1978. A more modern film was made in 2006 called *Superman Returns*, and a new film will be coming out in 2012 called *Superman: Man of Steel*.

The 2009 Batman film *The Dark Knight* made an incredible amount of money. It took $158 million (£99 million) at its opening weekend in US cinemas and £11 million in the UK.

Batman and the Joker in *The Dark Knight*.

IT'S AMAZING!

Between 2002 and 2007 three Spider-Man films were made. The first cost $138 million to make. The two following films were even more expensive, costing $200 million and $258 million!

Amazons a race of tall, strong and fierce female warriors in Greek mythology

arch-enemy a main enemy

armoured covered with or made of hard, protective metal

captor a person who takes someone else prisoner

cosmic rays waves from outer space

deflect to cause something to change direction

gadget a small tool or device with a clever design or unusual use

gamma ray a dangerous wave of energy

genetic mutation a change in a being before it is born that means it will look or act differently when it grows up

genius a person with an unusual ability to think or create

humanoid robots that have a human-like appearance or behaviour

insane crazy or mad

mineral a natural substance that comes from underground

nemesis someone that always works against you

radioactive giving off dangerous rays of energy

repulsor rays a weapon similar to a laser beam that can repel and injure enemies

secret identity a disguise that superheroes use to hide who they really are

storyboard a series of images that tell a story

supernatural coming from outside the natural world

Books

Action Heroes & Superheroes (21st Century Lives), Adam Sutherland, Wayland, 2010

Create Your Own Superhero Stories, Paul Moran, Buster Books, 2010.

Guardian of the Earth (Green Lantern), Michael Dahl, Stone Arch, 2011.

Superman: The Shadow Master (DC Super Heroes), Paul Kupperberg & Rick Burchett, Capstone, 2010.

Websites

Home of Marvel comics.
  http://marvel.com/
Home of DC comics.
  www.dccomics.com
Learn about all the different superheroes on the Superhero database.
  www.superherodb.com/

TV Series

Ben 10 (TV Series 2005–2007)
   Cartoon Network
Fantastic Four
   (TV Series 1994–1996)
The Incredible Hulk
   (TV Series 1996–1997)
The New Adventures of Superman
   (TV Series 1993-1997)
Transformers: Animated (TV Series 2007–)
Wolverine and the X-Men
   (TV Series 2008–)
X-Men: Evolution (TV Series 2000–2003)

INDEX

Banner, Dr Bruce 16–17

Batman 5, 14–15, 29

Ben 10 20–21

Bumblebee 26, 27

criminals 4, 7, 18, 20

DC comics 6–7

equipment 5, 12, 14, 17, 19

gadgets 5, 12, 14

Green Goblin 11

Human Torch, the 23

Invisible Woman, the 23

Joker, the 15, 29

Kent, Clark 8

kryptonite 9

Luthor, Lex 9

Marvel comics 6–7, 27

Mr Fantastic 22, 23

Nanomech 21

Optimus Prime 26

Parker, Peter 10

secret identities 5, 22

Spider-Man 4, 7, 10–11, 29

Stark, Tony 18–19

Storm 25

Superman 7, 8–9, 28

superpowers 4–5, 8, 10, 12, 16, 17, 20, 21, 22, 23, 24–25

Tennyson, Ben 20–21

Thing, the 23

Transformers 26–27

Wayne, Bruce 5, 14

Wolverine 24

Wonder Woman 12–13

Xavier, Charles 25